Kizziness

A state of silly craziness, wonder and awe, dancing in the rain,
joyful, unapologetic love for the amazingness of everything...

For the lovers
and dreamers
the broken Kintsugi
the philosophers
the prophets
the poets
the artists
the magicians
the amazing word alchemists
the sandcastle builders
the snow angel makers
the rain dancers
the roses and weeds
the strong and the weak
the moths and the butterflies
the naked, without skin
komorebi firefly souls
the worthy unloved and beloved
and wounded warriors
who wrote these words
on my heart again

In gratitude
I dedicate these poetries
To you

and

For
My Forever Beloved

the sacred words
"I love you,"

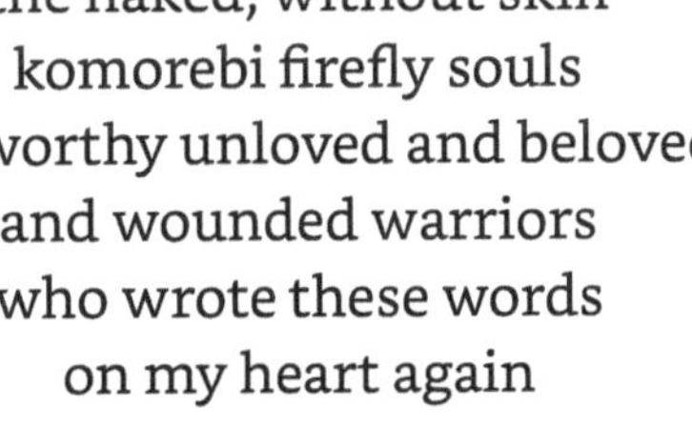

my last breath

Love Until It Breaks You, Again, and Again, and Again...

Special Thank You and Acknowledgment To:

My beloved Mother who died as I finished typing
the last pages of this Poetry Series,

And who taught me how to love.

My patient family and friends who never stop
loving, supporting, and encouraging me.

My Instagram friends, poets and community who
loved, supported, inspired and encouraged me.

My dear Abi for typing the first three volumes.

My Beloved who taught me what true love really means.

With Love And Gratitude

Until The End Of Forever

The Longing

Longing to belong
To someone who
Longs to belong
To someone, too,
Relentlessly, devotedly,
Unconditionally,
Unapologetically
In love

Saudade

It is the longing
That keeps me alive
Just to kill me everyday
And it never goes away

Web Weavers

Aerial gliders
Contortionists on silk threads
Weave beguiling snares

Tu Me Manques

Longing for one word from you
So I can believe
The world did not end
And love exists

Train of Thoughts

Longing for the light
At the end of the tunnel
To run me over
And end this longing

Your Last Poem

Salted acceptance
Final tear rolls down my face
Our love's eulogy

Abandoned Dreams

In an uneven chair at the station
Falling into resignation
Watching trains come and go
Picking up while dropping off
Those who never leave or stay
The haunting whistle blows
Another piece of me rolls away
As the train grows and grows
While the tracks grow shorter still
The void of ache to fill
Wishing on the stars
Above the endless empty cars
Where nothing's as it seems
In this place of abandoned dreams

If

If I told you that I love you
Could you, would you know,
What amazing sparks of heaven
Are created by your magnificent soul
In my heart's arms
Where we dance
In clouds of rain

As If

I used to stare at you for hours
To take in every nuance
Trying to memorize each moment
Your lips against my lips
Your smell of home
Your warm and tender touch
Your heart against my chest
Your breath against my neck
As if I could ever
Somehow forget

Love Is A Verb

Love is the greatest power in the universe.
Its your superpower.
Love is a verb
Go do it!

Magnificent Alchemy

You are the music in the silence
The light that breaks the clouds
The world in a drop of dew
On the tip of a blade of grass
At dawn's illumination
And still these words are meaningless,
You are simply magnificent alchemy
In a world that has abandoned true magic
And for that alone,
Even among the tall rainbows
Slicing prisms into vibrant truths,
For even this grace you are
I give thanks eternally
No matter how inadequate I am to express it
And so I say, "I love you,"
As if you can know
My heart's true meaning

Echoes

Sometimes late at night
I sense you in an odd way
That escapes comprehension
I reach across a thin veil for your hand
To entangle fingers, transparent
In the flickering candlelight
And recognize we are ghosts of distant fires
I can only breathe to life
With frozen sighs
Echoing unspoken love

Telegraphing

Telegraphing on warm July nights
In cars like boats, taking flight
Floating north to south
Windows all the way down
My hand out the window pushing down
Until I reached a smile
That accepted lift and flew
Until pulled down again
With some gravitational force
That screamed, "Again! Again!"
The street lights flickering
In nights so magic
Even wizards perched
At the corner of Nine Mile
As we sang along to WHNN
Into the shining parade
Before Motor City died

To The God Of Love And Grace

I pray this on my face,
I ask the God of love and grace,
To remove him from my heart
Or remove my heart, so torn apart,
Take this perfect love, this sacred truth,
Because, this is not fantasy,
Not romantic poetry,
And it hurts more than I can bear,
Too raw and real, in truth I swear,
He loves me still
And always will
He is just not brave enough
To love like this kind of love
Too sane to love with such treason
Of fierce intensity that defies all reason.

The Magicians Pen

The magician sat before the book
Its pages bright and clean
And as he felt
Each tear did melt
Into symbols neatly arranged
Side by side in spells perhaps
And potions long since estranged
He stroked his beard and found his pen
He'd misplaced some time ago
When overcome by sleep
That would not come or go
The pen itself overflowed
With memories
And tears he could not cry
Without regret
The paper let
The pen draw perfect skies
That changed the symbols into words
"Let sleeping bunnies lie."

Rise And Shine

Some people
Like the sun
Remind us to rise up
After the darkness
And be a light for others.

Tourniquet

Checking texts again
Tightening the tourniquet
Never stops the truth

Blue Flame

Bloodletting again
Setting fire to love's last hope
Blue flame tears of pain

Six Feet Under

In the end,
We see things with such clarity
Through tears of loss
Of love so pure
And excruciatingly beautiful
That even Gods could not recreate
Except maybe in the laughter
Of babes in slumber.
Such love can never really be destroyed
But only buried alive
Under six feet of sorrow
Eternally frozen
In hopeless hope

Collateral Damages

Of love and lust and things of the heart
We purge the dark vessels of what's torn apart
Tears and wine, blood of ink
We never gave our grace to drink
Of darker passions deeply entwined
Within the words we disposed of
For the rhymes

Stowaway

I can never unlove you
You have somehow managed to stowaway
In the part of my heart
That is unsinkable
Forever golden
Hidden in plain sight.
And even if every ship
Should suddenly sink
And somehow all the oceans dry
Into alien landscaped deserts,
I will still wait quietly
For you to write your heart in the sand
And I will scratch a heart beneath it.

The Wind In The Weed

When I kissed your face that day
Then flew away
Pretending to be
A dandelion seed
I knew I loved you then,
As I became that golden weed
And you became my wind

First Sight

Is it the sincerity
That captures me
The undisguisable innocence
Or that fearful searching in their eyes
For someone who will finally understand
And not hurt them this time?
Or just a hallowed moment
When I see
Maybe home?

Origami Dragons

What if we lay in the sun, in fields of gold
Stringing flowers into crowns, just for fun
Would lay there and let it just unfold
Would you stay or would you run?

If I touched you
And you closed your eyes
Just imagining scarlet skies,
Maybe brushed your hair
From your face, unaware,
And let my lips fall here and there,
Would you mind?
Would you care?

Would you sigh beneath
The origami dragons
Fighting elephants in wagons
Made of iridescent clouds
Would smile with me out loud?
Would you run away
Or maybe stay?

Still Shines

Still the light shines through the trees
The cold spring water slips though my fingers
And love, itself,
Slips through the iron bars
We wrap around our hearts
And lets the God of love and grace
Brush our tears from our face
And kiss our souls
As if we were more precious
Than all the treasures of the universe
When in fact
We are only sparks of light
From the love that somehow
Still manages to shine

Spring Born

Serendipity
Babies dreaming Spring to life
Butterfly skies bloom

When No One Is Watching

When no one is watching
I dance upon rooftops
And tiptoe from tree to tree
I feel that tickle in my soul
And suddenly, I'm free
To leap and roll
In rapturous light,
Dip and dive in flawless flight
I swoop and rise above the clouds
I live my life in truth, so loud
I write your name in stardust flame
Across the satin sky
In honor of the sacred love
That never ends or dies
When no one is watching me cry.

Objects In The Rear-View Mirror

I can still[see him
Silhouetted in the doorway
Looking like someone
Who would not be there
When I came back
From leaving him

Night's Eye

Night's eye sees though you
The moon hides all your secrets
Reflected bright lies

Just Saying

Who did you think I was, then,
A child in the street where you prey?
A peasant to buy with some candy,
A present to open when you want to play?
What made you think
I was low hanging fruit,
A hideous stink
To be wiped from your boot?
In fact, I'm amazing
I have never been dumb,
And you were a slum dog
Just sniffing for crumbs.

Pretend

I never had a choice in loving you
Never had a voice louder than this truth
Never felt and aching
Like my heart awakening
There was never an escape from your dark eyes
Never any shape to fill the void of sighs
Never any day I dreamed you'd run away
Never understood how you could
Never believed that you would
Blow it all away in the wind
Leaving wishes to pretend
Our love was as real
As you made it feel

Time's Door

Time ago and time again
I know I'd do it all again
Just to lay at your feet
To worship the ground where you stand
I would try not to cry
Knowing, goodbye,
Is how the story ends
And I would cling to your love
Like a a baby holds its mother.
I could never love another
But just pretend it never ends
And that moment just before,
I would crawl through time's door
And do it all again
And again
And again

Content Matters

What spell was broken
Enchanted words spoken
Whose resilient poetic refrains
Spawned monuments to all the remains

Ephemeral moments glare
Embellished with such flair
Shimmering brightly in serein
The magnificent masterful stain

Prismatic scattered shards
Casting rainbows from the scarred
The resplendent mellifluous shatter
Eloquent bewitched content matters

Was my heart really smashed
And my faith all but trashed
Did my blood flow from reopened scars
Painting blight into raptured stars?

Innocence bludgeoned
Met with high dudgeon
In archaic timeless revenge
A life left unhinged

Redamancy Pure

Let's slip through time's door
To the love we had before
And never look back
Let's linger at the gate
In wait for destined fate,
Mercy wrapped in grace
To spill a rainbow
From a crack in heaven's floor
Redamancy pure

Beyond Our Destiny

In a million galaxies
Reversing dimensions behind thin veils
Something whispers life into our sails
And so we navigate,
By breaths of unknown love
Until we become adrift
In seas of sovereign sacred
Beyond our destiny
Awakened

Big Love

Does a little love go a long way?
There is no little love
From a big heart!

Tears Lost

You redefine love
In ways I cannot name
Your heart speaks to me
And I hear it with my soul
In whispered words
Like tears lost in rain
Casting hopeful rainbows
From smiling pain

Kite

Find your joy
Let it soar above the clouds
In its graceful way
To find you looking up
To better days
And if the sun, so bright
Should burn your eyes
Don't let it take you by surprise
It's just the tears you never cried
For all those years
You forgot that you could fly

Verity

We are, each of us,
Poets and prophets,
Sinners and saints,
Divining wellsprings of hope
From desert sands
Of savage heat
Freezing with moon-rise
Fluid
We wipe our eyes
And speak our valiant hearts
In true validity
Seeking human kindness
And find the night is full of dangers
Waiting for our respite
In the shivering cacophony
Of life awakened
By instincts and hungers
Wild predators prey
While we pray
And still we rise
To face another day,
Arms outstretched
In gratitude
To those who gave us the strength
To make it through
The loud dark night,
To praise again the morning light.

Deadlines

Ever notice how nice people are to the dead?
Like they cross a line in their head
They bring flowers,
Sit for hours,
Water them with salty tears.
They share their day, for years
Hopes and prayers
Like someone's there
No one lies to the living
After they die
They bring flowers
Tell secrets for hours
Meant for lovers roun
In the moments before dawn

Lifelines

Even the smallest souls
Speak so much truth
In loving trust
And gentle presence

Deeply Loved

I love you
With a deeper understanding
Than my mind can communicate
I love you stronger
Than my heart
Can carry in silence

Deeper Exit Wounds

Darker places bleed
Deeper exit wounds within
What is friendly fire?

Petrichor Sigh

Komorebi woods
Serein musky moss drenched hush
Tree frog lullabies

Love IS A Verb

Love comes in many forms
To remind us to live
In truth and compassion,
You cannot give love
Without receiving
But don't do it for that reason

Wondering

The world awakens
To glorious sunrise,
Magnificent, majestic mountains
Shimmering with snow,
Miles of sparkling desert sands
Oasis of life bursting from darkness,
Smile and tear
The laughter of babes
And yet, somehow,
Humans think,
How superior I am to all of this
Irreverent innocuous beauty
Let's kill everything
That is less than us
And blow this paradise
Into oblivion.
I wonder in the wonder
Why?

Pieces of Offerings

He love me with such purity and innocence
I never felt I deserved his loving gaze,
His perfect heart,
And yet, like one who is dying
Of thirst and starvation,
I did feast at his table
The breath of his lips
Until the poison
Gave me peace

Out Of The Shallows

My spirit fluid,
Ethereal,
Powerful,
Humbled,
In awe of all that is,
Sings softly to the sea
Dances upon the lacy waves
Elysian lights that leap
To meet my feet
Hoovering the deep

Good Mornings and Good Nights

After darkness follows dawn
After storms, follows rainbows
What art is this made manifest
In resilience and faith?
Look inside,
It is your soul.

Remember We

Move within the mountains
In the sleeping snow crested ravines
Sail upon the windless ghosts of waters
Through sculptured chiseled caverns
Leaving sparks of us
Within the cloudless skies
Remember we
Eternally

Resolute

I love to watch the earth
Shift subtly into wistful night
And wonder
What will be different
In the morning light
I know it won't be me

Thank You

Curled up in my blanket
Mostly to numb to cry
The tears just riding the waves
Inside of the storm
I can't navigate anymore
I feel their fingers
Dancing on the keys
And the music of the poetry
Is in my heart, soothing me
Like a friend
That strokes my hair, saying,
"Everything will be okay"
Holding my pieces together
And they don't even know it

KIZZINESS ROSE

The Smell Of Rain

God made rain
Smell like you

Rise

Spark the hallowed blaze
Let the ash flow through your wings
Sanctified by flame

Even the Lion

Some people never realize
Even the lion is carried
Dragged along
By innocent wisdom,
Fierce devotion,
Loving arms
We cannot see,
Watching the past
Fade behind us.

Be Kind

Kindness,
Like a breath of divinity,
Rises up from the darkest places
To lift us above our deepest sorrows
Restoring our soul

Phantom Pain

Tu me manques toujour
You are missing from me always
I'll never be free

Saudade Rain

My ghost soul mirrored in your eyes
Smooth puddles of fresh rain
Beneath the blackest skies
Where heavens wept in vain

I lay in hope of peace
The asphalt ice so warm beneath
The wish of more than empty streets
I did my shattered heart bequeath

To all that was and maybe dreamed
Soul bloodshed filled deep drains
The silence of the censored screamed
To and of the love that still remains

The Warrior Kneels

Each new day is such a gift,
We wait for night's dark veil to lift
The warrior kneels again in praise
To rise to love another day.

Tear Garden

Well-tended wasteland
Sorrow grows from these gardens
Love dies beneath stone

Stick-People Wordless True

Ineffable confession
Redundant by Repression

I love you and miss you
Stick-people wordless true

The sun speaks in rhythmic sighs
While aberrant waves' refrains belies

And I think of you in cloud heirophants
Riding marshmallow elephants
Through cotton caverns glazed in golden hue
This love was made of magic made untrue

I lay my sparkling heart at your feet
Fearful our souls' eyes would meet,
Then run as far as infinity allows
Unafraid, undeterred, I disavow
The notion I will never hold you
Or this love, itself, could not be true

Magnificent Lights

I have stood beneath them
All the magnificent lights,
The shimmering stars,
Nebulae, constellations,
Auroras
All the phases of the moon,
Just wondering
What artist's hand could dream
Imagine, create such poetry
Such, beauty, such magic
As these
And deeply understood
The universal God of love and grace
At such a level
That my tears could not give justice.
I fell to my knees
And embraced truth...

Love is real

Sanguinolency

Unhinged
Untangling knots
Unraveling barbed bonds
Unsnarling unrelenting unrequited love
Unchained

Mangata

After midnight breathes
Floating in fallen moon seas
Starry-skied secrets

The Heart You Buried

If tomorrow comes
And life is still
Water-colored wonder
Will you still pretend
It's black and white
Pen and ink line art,
To unbreak the heart
You buried in your bullshit?

I Hope You Find This

Haiku confession
Left on a tattered napkin
"I've always loved you"

Radiance

Every hole in a massive sign
Made for artificial lights
Above a modern business
Over a hundred feet wide
Contains a small bird with a nest
There has never been anything
But natural light and music
From this man-made structure
Life springs from it
And always sings from this
Perfectly designed habitat
Unaware in elegant synchronicity
For this natural phenomenon
Of serendipitous wonderment
Of opportune potentials
As we all are

It is our holes
Not artificial light
That make us holy
That make us shine

Dance

Dance with me
Beneath the stars
And never let go

Midnight Train

Same train whistles howls
Rumbling through the midnight woods
Lost friends call me home

A Bridge Of Hope

Our love built a bridge
Across oceans between us
Tethering our hearts

Unfazed

Watched you slip away
On a bridge of my soul's tears
Frozen by disdain

Sawdust

Lost another friend
Seemed inevitable
It would end
Sawdust escaping empty breaths
Made me wish for death.
Tell me something real
Like how you feel
Not just your lists
Of dreams and needs
Show me where
You really bleed
Of just fall back asleep
With all the other sheep
Leave me in the deep.
Arms you ask to hold you
Only mold you
Into compliance
Rediscovered self-reliance
In tears of silence
Call me when you find your voice
Your algorithmic choice
Is it about the love or only fame?
Follow, like and save
And stay the same.

Moonlighting

Sometimes late at night
I hear the light whispering
Stars dance on its breath

Real Love Is Not Temporary

Love you until the end of forever
NOT just until it becomes socially unacceptable to
Because you ghost me
Or I find someone better

Love is not what you say,
Love is what you do.

Unbreakable

I am so fragile
Already broken
Particles of vapor
Frozen tears unshed
Tomorrow's game called for rain
Unaccredited pain
Dragged behind painted horses
Uncertain of clay-dust visions
In the sunset
Warrior statues wait to be unearthed
I am not strong
But still unbreakable
Because of the size
Of what remains

Perfect Sacrifice

I wish that all these tears
Were Diamond pearls
I would lay then at your feet
And bury my defeat
In all that perfect sacrifice
Of these pieces of my soul

Path Etiquette

I lay here where you left me
Along your path of non-goodbyes
Buried in the memories
Of all you well-worn lies
I am not some weed grown from a crack
I am meld in this place
Of don't look back

Post Mortem Ghost Written

My beloved,
Heart of my heart,
Soul of my soul,
I surrender.
The words,
"I love you,"
My last breath.

I will say the word
You cannot

Goodbye

The Absence

I've written so much
Inside my head
But not on paper
I reach a point of things unsaid
I let them live there, instead,
In that space of silence.
The silence so cold, so deafening
When I became ghosted,
Until the silence became peace.
Silenced, I stopped speaking.
Now it seems like
I am losing my hearing, too.
I wonder if the silence
Is just the absence of noise.

Heartbreak

Welcome to my heartbreak
Is it more than you can take?
Tell me why I can't say, "Hi"
and you can't say "Goodbye?"
Why are you incapable of tears
And I have not stopped crying all these years?
What is that soul-quaking
Sound of one heart breaking?
A crack in reality
Leading to insanity
A loss of Fantasy
Regarding your humanity

Ondinnonk

Numinous trouvaille
Ondinnonk orenda
Orphic nepenthe

Overwhelming awe-filled serendipitous love,
Soul dreamed mystical, life-changing force,
Mysterious healer of my grief-stricken heart.

I Would

I would if I could
Shelter you
That you always live
Where angels dwell
For lack of awe for anything
But your beautiful soul
And your every precious breath.
I would,
If I only could.

As Wonder Evolves

As abundance become wonder
Revealing true colors
Unveiled of facade
The fire of truth
Painting beauty on life
Before shedding
What no longer serves it
Creating space for renewal
As wither becomes wonder evolved
Endlessly

The Quiet

Sometimes it's so quiet
You can hear a pen drop
Sometimes the pen
Spills the poetry to the page
Like the blood of my veins
Flowing directly
From my heartbreak
Purified by silence

And Still I Kneel

Defiant love
Pledges fealty to thee
On bended knee
Seeking only that great treasure
Beating beneath thy armored breast
I would melt away with true love's tears
If not for miles and years
And still I kneel
For renewal
And good tidings of hope
Beyond simple measures
Of misspoken lies
In whispered truths
As such are legends woven.

Return to Cinder

In these soft hours
Of darkening skies
And heavy sighs
Echoing tenderness
Falls upon my soul
Where tenderness left a hole
Where once I was whole
The tender becomes tinder
As I surrender
Shredded words
Returned to sender
Among the embers
Returns to cinder

Tree Of Dreams

An ancient tree
With many storms endured
Deep secrets held
And seasons passed
With changes forged in grace.
Arms outstretched to touch stars
Strong roots have dug so deep
That it remains a sturdy force
Anchored in abundant faith
Branches, above, roots below,
A mirror image.
Both darkness and light sustain,
Within them both,
It evolves, and remains.
Living things find shelter here
In welcoming embrace
Alone within a forest of dreams
Forever a breath away
From your beloved
Unreachable soul

And Still I Love

You took my breath
In just one heart stopping moment
You stole my heart forever
Hypnotic force of nature
My sanity lost
My body surrendered
My soul entwined in yours
There's nothing left of me
But tears
You can't return
This unrelenting love

Unnatural Disaster

What is this mysterious force of nature
To circumvent the hurricane,
Contain the earthquake,
Forestall the volcanic inevitable acceptance
Yet, unable to release
That soft sigh of resignation
That we are not loved,
Within a tear
From the eye of the storm?

Listen

Life is an epic poem,
A deep ethereal song,
An ever-changing canvas
Of an ever-evolving painting,
A continual conversation
Between and artist and your soul.
Listen...

Life is an epic poem,
A deep ethereal song,
An ever-changing canvas
Of an ever-evolving painting,

Fading

Fading photographs
Crisp cotton sheet clothesline dried
Sun-baked memories

Saudade Tide

Crashing empty shores
My heart keeps pounding like waves
Endlessly breaking

Rivened

Riven scintilla
Drifting winds of lava sparks
Stirred in solitude

Savage Love

Should every star
Fall into black holes
Remaining from the agony
Of true love's loss,
Savage love,
So rare and magnificent
That it tears the very fabric of the universe,
Its absence being heavier
Than heaven's gravity,
I will still love.
And I will still love you.

Unchained

Corralled charismatic
Choirs of angels chant
Chorus of chosen carols
Unchained, the poet dances
With cymbals of symbols
Creating symbiotic symphonies
In solitude's soliloquy
Sauntering salacious sovereignty
Serene in the serein

Fallen Star Wish

Moonlit love's embrace
Falling-star wish grants first kiss
Love's spell on my skin

Beautiful Trash

My heart, poured out each day
Into old bottles
In effort to give justice
To my soul's gentle whisperings
For my love so far
And crashed against hidden rocks,
Beaten by heavy waves,
In squalls of screaming pain,
Shattered, scattered,
Sharp edges worn soft
Shards of what is left
Of the discarded
Unwanted, unloved,
Well-worn beautiful trash
I am sea glass

Shine

Charisma
Day breaks
Blinding bright truth
Spirit light shines through
Radiance

Haunted

How do I pretend
From this chair that I've become
That I'm still alive

How do I pretend
From this chair that I've become
That I'm still alive

Win Win

Fight for each other
Not against
I can't win
If you lose
I can't lose
If you win

Word Ballet

Your words dance
In chaotic glamour
Like a sudden spring storm
That leaves it's scent
Long after the mud-puddled
Choreographed echoes

Painfully Numb

White-capped beach shivers
Veiled wisps of dragon mists glow
Winter tastes my blues

Wonder

Pastel winter skies
Frost breaths of miserere
Whispered angel's sighs

Walk With Me

Walk with me
Among the diamond dust snow,
Deeper into the forest
Where the moonlight spills glitter
In the softness of the sacred,
Hold my hand in the hallowed wonder,
The gentle magic whispering
Holy, in a perfect moment of purity
Between earth and sky
Heart and soul
Awe-struck raptured love

Secret Storm

My heart is bursting
Love, desire, passion's fire
How can I tell you?

Happily Ever Afterthoughts

Cognitive dissonance
Unrequited love
Can love be quieted?

Unconditional, eternal love
Let it go, walk away
If they change their mind

Unshakable flexibility
Fragile resilience,
Drunk love,
Silent love,
Painful Poisoned Passion

What is this dissonance
That dissolves our resolve?
Beautiful lies,
Happily ever afterthoughts

Komorebi Hymn

My beloved
Nourish me
Warm me with you grace
That you could find a place for me
Within your perfect heart
That bleeds poetry
Arias of Angels
In your innocent eyes
Of wonder and purity.
A heart so sacred as this
I would find my home
My release
In such euphoric cries
The world would be silent
But for this Komorebi Hymn
Deep within the ethereal forest

Hopeless Faith

Binaural beats
Of long tendrilled sunlight
Cast blue shadows
Where giants once lumbered in silence
Fragmented frozen sands
A misplaced hourglass
Splintered with hopeless faith.

Your Eyes

When I saw your eyes
Love filled my being with light
Dissolving his lies

Look Up

The God of love and grace
Would tell you to your face,
How beautiful you are,
Bright and brilliant star,
When drinking from this cup,
Look up, dear one,
Look up

Let It Rain

Still it comes like hard rain
That dissolves my deepest pain
With every drop upon my skin
Everywhere, erupting from within

Nothing else could free me
No one else could see me
Let me be me
The thought of you fills every empty space
No one, nothing can replace

Wash it all away
All the darkest days
Let it pour down from above
Let the sky drench me in love
And let it grow the things
The thought of you brings
The new song my heart sings

The Calm

It was only in the middle
Of the calm black sea
Alone on a balcony
Deep into the darkest night
Did I understand,
The storm was always in me
And I was the calm in it

The Perfect Wave

Life is often
The slow turning of a ship
To climb the wall of black water
To sit atop an endless rogue wave
For a breathless moment
And ride that mountain
Like a surfboard
Sliding into calm, breathlessly,
Eternally searching
For that next perfect wave.

Beyond Just This Day

Crush me with desire
Consume me in your fire
Enraptured by your perfect heart
But decide before you start
My love is yours to own
It's not on loan
Love me beyond just this day
Make it real
Or go away
I don't play
If you want me,
Stay

My Forever Valentine

His eyes were the hues
Of summer sand sand black sea,
Sea glass treasures
Shimmering in passion's heat.
His mouth defined ecstasy in rhapsody
Wild explosive crescendos
Pounding in my heart.
I dreamt him in a seashell moment
Drenched in sweat
Refusing to wash the heat
In the cool dark oceans of his eyes
With fusion blessed starlight
Among the dreams of his sweet kiss
Forever my Valentine

Tethered

Tether me to your heart
Let me climb into the clouds
Swooping and diving in the winds
Dancing with the birds
Sailing seas of sky in every hue
Run with me
Dance with me
Watch my fragile heart
Climb into the heavens
Tethered to your soul
Then reel me in
Back to your heart
Let me dance inside your soul
I want to go home

Somnolence

Unbreakable urn
Ashes of love that once burned
Sealed heart, overturned

Unreasonable

Bitter Seasoning
Wanton Disillusioning
Treason's Reasoning

I See You

A blessing can be felt and never seen
Because, in divine truth,
You are blessed
Without need for sight,
Because such things live in a place
Where they can only be seen by the heart.
Even my soul sees
What my eyes can never imagine,
That is how I see you

Truth

Snowflake butterflies
Carrying away my poems
White chalked rice paper

Peace On Earth

White-tailed frozen fawn
Between rows of iced glass trees
Sacred glow of dawn

Intertwined

I reach out my hand
Entangling my fingers in yours
And forget that we will never touch
In this existence
For a moment that trembles
With the epiphany
That our souls
Have never been apart

Pluperfect

You are the light
Reflected from the perfect lotus
Growing in the humble stillness of mud
Content to shine resilient splendor
Pure, in elegant grace
Every dawn

Sacrosanct

I exist in worlds that intersect my soul
In clandestine splendor of sunlit smiles
Echoing tenderness and love
In whispered memories
Awakened in the sacred now
Of this perfect holy moment
Eternally

The Placeholder

Does anyone love the coat on the chair
Or the heart hoping there
The neatly folded card on the table
That saves a space reserved
For those who can be loved?

Defenestration

It was once a custom of Scandinavian people
To open a window for the dying
So that their souls can get out.
I have been passing the open windows
For so long, crawling,
Slipping and sliding,
In my own tears and blood,
Over the sharp broken pieces
Of what is left of me
That I have forgotten how to fly.

Without Shame

What is the currency of love?
Is it a kiss deeply savored,
A touch of a cheek
Warmed and pressed against a chest,
A heart-stopping, time altering gaze
Into another's soul, amazed?
Or a stoic clock ticking
Above wilted flowers for years?
The seas are full of God's tears,
Still, I rage against the gray
Every day
To drown in raptured sunsets,
A beggar without shame

At Cause

She saw the light in his eyes
And let it fill her heart so full
That she forgot how to be sad
That he could never love her

Disparagement

Sarcasm
Passive aggression
To tear flesh
"Have a nice day!"
Sanguinolency

Possessed

And then I saw it in his eyes
That spark of the entire universe
That owns my soul

Your Blood Beats My Heart

You deserve to be loved by someone
To such a degree that your souls
Have no boundaries
Their breath is your breath
You hearts entwine so inseparable
That even your blood beats their heart
Loved without reservation
Unapologetically, unconditionally, enduring,
Unashamed to lay at your feet
To cherish even your presence
As sacred, holy, divine.
You always deserve to be loved in this way.
You are not disposable
You are not an option
A placeholder for someone deemed worthy
You have always been worthy
You have always been a priceless treasure
You are worthy of only this purity of love
Only this is true love
Only this love is worthy of you.

If You Knew Me

You judge me harshly
Like you know me
You slice me open
Like a piece of raw meat
Like I deserve it
For not living up to your expectations
As if I refuse
To be good enough for you
Don't threaten me with consequences
For standing up for myself
While you accuse me
Of things you made up
To prove to yourself
I am not good enough
Who are you to judge me
Like you know me?
If you knew me
You wouldn't judge me
You would know
I love you

The Hum Of Evening

Cars on distant highways sail
Beneath silent asteroids,
Low rumbling of our mother's hunger
For Dawn's watercolor skies,
Car headlight music hums,
Rolling briefly by,
Into unknown journeys.
Mothers' gentle cradle songs
Compete with lovers' lullabies
Into the deep hours of wordless
Thunderous , love struck night arias
Lost in your starlight eyes

A Breath Away From Bliss

I once touched a star
Pulled it close enough to kiss
Lingering in its complexities
Until it became clear
In the stark realization of love.
I once caressed a star
A breath away from a kiss
So many light years away
Mesmerized in eternal bliss,
Until nothing could ever touch
That space in my soul again
Without causing anguish
Nothing but that nebula
Exploding hallowed endlessly
Embraced to my heart
Unwilling and unable
To untangle

The Dissonance Of Trust

Qualia
Explanatory gap
Ineffable raw feelings
Undefinable conceived personal truths
Perceptions

Heartless

If you had taken my heart
Instead of my mind,
Plucked out my eyes
And just left me blind,
Cut off my ears
So I couldn't hear,
I wouldn't,
I couldn't
Have cried all these years.

PretEND

The harsh difference
Between true love and pretend
Is found in the end

Poetry Is Love

I want to lay on a blanket
In the cool evening
Beneath a shade tree
And stare across our notebooks
Full of poetry and ramblings
And smile, in silence.
Every now and again
To brush your cheek
and softly wipe your tired eyes,
and leave my palm against your lips
Until you kiss it,
And then hold it to my heart.
Sighing as the wind blows my pages,
Rustling my scrambled thoughts
As I fall into your dark eyes,
Wandering and wondering
At all the volumes I haven't read
Or blank pages writing their selves,
As the sunlight casts shadows on your face
I'll hold my breath,
Waiting...
Waiting...

Tender The Shadows

Tender the shadows that fall on the space
So void of the everything I cannot replace
Tender the fire that warmed our embrace
Casting shadows in valleys
Our bodies once graced.
Tender the tinder,
While in the soft glow
Hold on to the shadows of love
Don't let go.

Love Until It Breaks You
Again And Again And Again

Love until it breaks you
Shakes you, 'til it wakes you
Let the heartbreak recreate you
Body, mind and soul
Love like you'll never love again
Broken, scared, destroyed, and then
Love Until It Breaks You
Again And Again
And Again...